Creative Design In
SAND CASTING

Techniques in Plaster, Cement, and Glass
for Making Wall Plaques and Standing Sculptures
by Carla and John B. Kenny

CROWN PUBLISHERS, INC., NEW YORK

Also by Carla and John B. Kenny
The Art of Papier Mâché
Design in Papier Mâché

Also by John B. Kenny
The Complete Book of Pottery Making
Ceramic Sculpture
Ceramic Design

Inquiries should be addressed to
Crown Publishers, Inc.,
One Park Avenue,
New York, N.Y. 10016

Printed in the United States of America

Published simultaneously in Canada by General Publishing Company Limited

Book Design: Huguette Franco

Library of Congress Cataloging in Publication Data

Kenny, Carla.
    Creative design in sand casting.

    1.   Sand casting.   I.   Kenny, John B., joint author.
II.   Title.
TT295.K46   1978   738.1'42   77-14582
ISBN 0-517-52948-3
ISBN 0-517-52949-1 pbk.

Contents

Introduction

Remember when you were a child and built sand castles on a beach or in a nursery school sandbox? That was when your career as a sand caster began.

For many, sand casting suggests a foundry and the shaping of metals for industry as has been done since tools and weapons of iron were first made. But sand casting is also an art form. The beautiful bas-reliefs on the doors of the cathedrals of Europe and this country were created by sand casting, and so were most of the classical pieces of metal sculpture.

The next time you visit the seashore, walk at the water's edge and notice the fine-line "drawings" left as each wave subsides and the next overlaps slightly higher or lower on the sand. Study those lovely lines and you will see mountains, dunes, cloud forms—all drawn by the gentle waves. Also be aware of the accidental designs of nature made by the footprints of birds and people. Notice the beauty of the sand itself—its color, its texture caused by tiny particles of crustaceans, of coral, granite, or quartz.

Sand is a valuable material for the artist and the craftsman. It has almost limitless possibilities. Modeling in sand, one designs in reverse by digging down instead of building up the way one makes sand castles. Such design in reverse is called *intaglio*.

You too can create by this process. With some imagination and a bit of practice you will be able to make bas-relief plaques for exterior or interior walls, free-standing sculpture, additions to room dividers, even interesting and exciting lighting effects.

Sand casting is an inexpensive craft. Most of the tools needed are in your kitchen right now. Other things such as pigments and brushes and modeling tools can be bought from local arts and crafts stores. Plaster of paris

Plate 1. Trilobite, an anthropod from the Paleozoic Era, in a "sand casting" made about 500 million years ago and found in West Georgia, Vermont. Photograph courtesy of the American Museum of Natural History, New York.

←

(and sand, if you are not near a beach or a desert) you will buy from building-supply dealers.

The first sand castings ever made are the fossils created by Mother Nature in ocean beds many millions of years ago. Some of those ocean beds are now dry land—in fact, most of the United States used to be at the bottom of a sea. The trilobite shown here was found in West Georgia, Vermont. It is about 500 million years old. Visit a museum of natural history when you have a chance, to enjoy the beauty of some of these prehistoric imprints of plant and animal forms.

Now, let's go to work.

On The Beach 1

W e shall begin our romance with sand casting by making a casting from a pressing in sand at the seashore.

Needed: A bag of plaster of paris (molding plaster)
A plastic mixing bowl
A pail for fresh waer
Blocks of wood
A large plastic spoon
Small plastic picnic utensils (knife, fork, spoon)
Picture wire (cut in 6″, 10″, and 12″ lengths)
A paring knife
A stiff hairbrush or whisk broom
A plastic spray bottle (filled with fresh water)
The bottom half of a quart milk container
A measuring cup
And don't forget—beach towels, beach umbrella, folding chair

PHOTO SERIES   1   *Sandy Hands*

1. Our materials are assembled, fresh water is in the bucket, a few shells have been gathered.

2. A rectangular depression has been made in the sand using the block of wood. The artist's right hand makes a pressing. (To make the impression deep enough the other hand must help by adding pressure on top.)

3. The left hand has made an impression in similar fashion. The plastic fork is used to introduce texture into the design by stroking the tines gently through the moist sand. (Small shells are dropped into the hand imprints—colorful side down in the sand.)

PLASTER OF PARIS

Let's pause here for a moment or two to talk about this remarkable substance, plaster of paris. It is made by heating gypsum rock (alabaster). This rock is hard when it is dug from the ground, but the heating drives off the chemically combined water (or water of crystallization) which gives the rock its crystalline form. The heated gypsum is soft enough to be scratched with a fingernail. When the heated rock has been crushed into a fine white powder, we have a material which, when mixed with water, will crystallize (set) into a hard white mass resembling the original rock.

MIXING PLASTER

For production work, the proportions of plaster and water must be accurately measured. Mold makers use 2¾ lbs. of plaster to 1 qt. of water. However, for our work, such precision is not necessary, and since we are working on the beach and have no scale, we can measure by cupfuls, using 2¾ cups of plaster to 2 cups of water—or better still, we can mix the plaster "by eye" by sprinkling plaster into the water until it forms an island above the surface of the water. We must *sprinkle* it in.

SLAKING

After the plaster has been sprinkled into the water, it should remain undisturbed for at least two minutes. This period of slaking is important; stirring too soon will form lumps. After two minutes, stir.

STIRRING

Stirring is best done with a long-handled spoon of wood or plastic. (A stainless steel spoon can be used, but be sure to take extra care in cleaning it.) The stirring should be done with the spoon touching the bottom of the container. The container can be lifted slightly and banged down onto the beach to drive bubbles to the surface. Stirring should continue for two or three minutes; by that time the plaster will begin to thicken. When it has the consistency of medium heavy cream it is ready to pour. (Don't pour plaster before it starts to thicken. Plaster that is too liquid will ruin your design.)

4. Our mixing bowl has been two-thirds filled with fresh water. (There's a shower and faucet on the beach for bathers.) Plaster is sprinkled into the water—this must be done quickly.

5. Plaster is sprinkled in until an island forms above the surface of the water. When there is an island of plaster about 3″ in diameter, sufficient plaster has been used.

POURING

In sand casting, plaster must be poured smoothly and gently. It is often good to spoon plaster into intricate portions of the design. When delicate portions have been covered, continue by pouring plaster into the bowl of the spoon so that it can overflow gently.

6. The plaster was allowed to slake for two minutes and then was stirred for two minutes more until it started to thicken. Now plaster is being spooned into areas of the design.

7. Continuing to pour. A large plastic container filled with plaster is sometimes awkward to handle, so a portion of a milk carton is used as a small disposable pitcher. Plaster was dipped out of the mixing bowl and is now poured into the bowl of the large spoon so that it can be allowed to flow gently over the entire design.

8. The design has been completely covered with a layer of plaster; the piece of picture wire twisted to form a hanging loop is inserted.

9. The last bit of plaster is spooned out of the mixing bowl. The casting must now be left undisturbed until it sets.

SETTING

After plaster has been poured, it starts to thicken until it reaches the consistency of cream cheese (what we call the *cheese state*). If you wish to sign your casting, now is the time to scratch your name and the date into the plaster with a pointed tool or a pencil.

As plaster sets it gives off heat—becomes warm, almost hot, to the touch. As soon as the setting action is complete the plaster starts to cool; when it becomes completely cold (about thirty minutes, but we allow forty, just to be sure), the casting can be lifted out of the sand.

10. Forty minutes later. Sand has been pushed away from the edge of the casting on four sides so that the artist can reach under and lift the piece gently.

11. Casting has been turned over. The artist brushes away some of the sand.

12. A sea bath—the casting is strong enough now to be taken into the waves and scrubbed. (The artist wears a sheer drip-dry shirt as protection against the hot sun.)

13. The final casting.

Undersea panel 32″ long. The frame was made of four strips of red wood; flattened glass marbles were used for bubbles.

Mermaid beside a pool. The starfish in her hand and the seahorse in her hair are real.

Cityscape.

Angel plaque with stained glass halo.

Jeweled night light.

Sun-moon flirtation made of cement.

Bird on a wheel.

Plaque with rectangular areas of stained glass catching the afternoon sun.

Above:
Fish made of cement.

Below:
Rooster plaque.

Fun with a piece of driftwood (26" tall). →

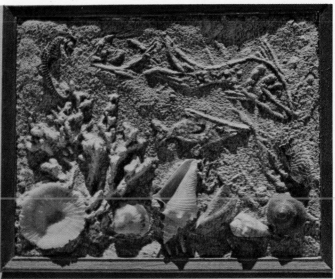

Above:
Snail on a garden fence.

Below:
Undersea plaque poured within a frame. Coral and shells were embedded deeply in the sand so that in the finished plaque they stand out in high relief.

← Stained glass abstract.

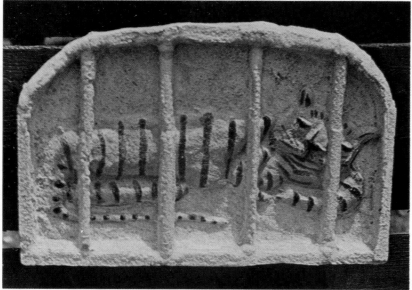

Above:
Three birds.

Below:
Tiger in a cage, painted with acrylics.

Plaque—dancing children. →

Amazon.

Stained glass abstract.

← Plaque—undersea scene.

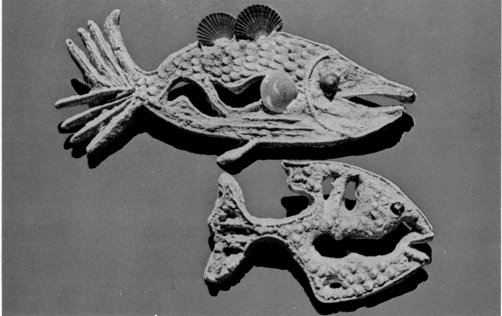

Above:
Glass-eyed fish.

Below:
Two fish, open sculptural forms.

→

Clown.

ENOUGH PLASTER?

After a little experience you will have learned how much plaster will be needed for any design you have prepared. If you find that you have run out of plaster before the casting is complete, no problem; just mix up another batch of plaster in the same container (without rinsing it) and carry on to completion.

PHOTO SERIES 2   *A Design Drawn And Scooped Out*

1. An area has been flattened and tamped firmly with the block of wood so that the mass of sand becomes quite compact. The outline of a fish is drawn with the blade of a plastic knife.

2. Scooping out the body of the fish with a large plastic spoon.

3. Using the plastic spoon to compact the scooped-out area.

4. Even though we work on the beach, where the sand is moist, sand dries out quickly under the hot sun, so from time to time the water sprayer is used to keep the sand moist. The design has been carried further here. A shell has been placed where the eye of the fish will be; another shell is in place to serve as a fin.

5. Texturing with a plastic fork. This is done by pressing and dragging the tines slowly over the surface of the sand.

6. More modeling. A small plastic spoon was pressed into the back of the fish to form scales, and here the knife is used to draw a mouth.

7. Plaster has been mixed. A small quantity is poured into the cut-down milk carton.

8. Starting to fill the design with plaster. The large spoon is used to pour plaster on the delicate design areas. It can be seen that the artist is suddenly working without benefit of sunlight. The sky turned black and it started to rain. Her assistant held a large beach umbrella over her while she completed the pouring. (Rain would have ruined the freshly poured plaster.) As soon as the pouring was finished, the storm became so fierce that the beach umbrella was wrested from the assistant's grasp and was blown out to sea. The artist had to protect her work by crouching over it like a mother hen shielding a baby chick. Fortunately, the story has a happy ending; the beach umbrella was rescued, the casting hardened without damage—

9. —and here it is. The finished casting. Note the use of shells for eye, fins, and teeth.

PHOTO SERIES 3 *Seahorse*

1. An area of moist sand has been compacted, and the shape of a seahorse has been scooped out. Here, sides of the depression are compacted by hand—the fingerprints form part of the design.

2. The design has been completed, and a shell has been put in place to serve as an eye; another shell has been inserted to form the back fin.

3. Some plaster has been carefully spooned into the design and then poured. Because of its shape, this figure will need some reinforcing. Here a piece of armature wire is inserted in the tail. (Armature wire is made of soft aluminum so that it can easily be bent into any desired shape. It can be bought in craft shops. Picture wire will do, but armature wire is slightly heavier and better for a piece of this sort.)

4. Disposable plastic knives are good for reinforcing. Here such a knife is pressed into the form. Note the wire hanging loop in the head.

5. Spooning the final bit of plaster.

6. Before the plaster hardens, the edge of the shape can be trimmed with a paring knife.

7. The outline of the tail has been trimmed. Here excess plaster under the jaw is cut away.

8. The seahorse has been bathed and scrubbed.

9. The finished casting.

The Home
Studio 2

If you are not fortunate enough to have an ocean in your front yard, you can still do casting in your garage or your patio or even in your living room. You will, of course, need to get some sand and have containers to hold it.

SAND

If you are near enough to a beach to be able to bring a couple of buckets of sand home with you, that is fine. If not, you may have to buy some.

One of the joys of sand casting is learning the differences that exist in this most abundant material. Sand from two different beaches can be quite different in texture, color, and character. Even on the same beach, walk a hundred yards along the shore in either direction and you'll probably find differences in the texture in the sand.

Now, how about buying sand?

BUYING SAND

Craft shops sell sand, usually in bags containing five or ten lbs. They also sell colored sand in 1-lb. plastic bags. But if you wish to do a lot of sand casting, you will find it much cheaper to buy your sand from a dealer in building supplies. They sell sand by the truck load, but if you will go to their storage yards with a 10-gallon plastic trash pail with a lid, you will, in almost every case, be able to buy a bushel of sand (about 50 lbs.), just enough to fill the pail, for less than a dollar. Your covered pail makes an excellent storage bin.

KINDS OF SAND

Building supply dealers all sell what is called *all-purpose sand,* which has been washed and screened and is just right for the artist sand caster.

Another type of sand is called *mason sand*, or *silica sand*. This is almost pure white and very fine.

A SANDBOX

The aluminum containers in which coffee cakes are sold are excellent for small work. For larger pieces you can buy aluminum baking pans 18″ x 14″ x 3″ or larger. This is the handiest size of all, for it can be put on a table top and easily moved out of the way if it rests on a tray. It can be easily stored.

THE EXECUTIVE SANDBOX

For larger work you may have to construct a box. We have made what we call *the executive sandbox* 24″ x 36″ x 2″, lined with Con-Tact paper, with executive rollers, as shown in Plate 2. We put this one on rollers because it would be too heavy to lift when filled with sand and if you wanted to put it to one side, it could easily be rolled under a table or even under the bed.

Now to work!

Plate 2a and b. Executive sandbox.

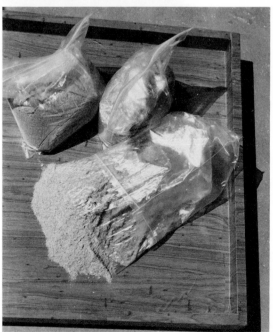

PHOTO SERIES 4 *A Simple Abstract Design*

1. Our aluminum baking dish has been filled almost to the top with sand brought from the beach. Unfortunately sand taken from a public beach may contain such things as burnt matches, cigarette butts, and pop can tabs, as well as rather large fragments of shells—such sand must be screened before we use it. A coarse strainer is used here and a large long-handled spoon.

2. The block of wood is used to make a rectangular depression.

3. The sand must be kept moist but not sopping wet. The spray bottle is used.

4. The sand must be compacted—the retaining wall is pressed with the fingers so it won't crumble into the plaster during the pouring. Doing this with the fingers gives us the feel of the sand. If it doesn't pack neatly, it is too dry—spray it some more.

5. Beginning to create a design with a plastic picnic knife pressed into the sand.

6. Completing the design with a plastic spoon.

7. Plaster was mixed in our plastic bowl. A small quantity was poured into a cheese container to make the pouring of the plaster easier. A plastic spoon is used to begin the pouring. (Plaster is heavy, and careless pouring can ruin a delicate design.)

8. Pouring plaster into the spoon so that it may flow gently over the design.

9. Inserting the hanging loop made of picture wire.

10. A second cupful of plaster completes the pouring.

11. After the plaster has crystallized (hardened) and becomes completely cool, the casting is lifted up and turned over. Rubbing a hand over the casting removes some of the wet sand.

12. Brushing off excess sand with a whisk broom.

13. The completed casting.

GOOD HOUSEKEEPING

In our home studio we don't have a convenient ocean in which to rinse our castings, but they can be hosed off in the backyard. Tools must be rinsed in a bucket of water and wiped dry. A strainer should be swished in a bucket of water so that sand that is dislodged can settle to the bottom of the bucket. When the washup is finished, water in the bucket can be carefully poured off and the sand remaining in the bottom can be wiped up with a damp newspaper and disposed of.

DISPOSING OF WASTE PLASTER

NO PLASTER MUST BE ALLOWED TO GET INTO THE SINK. If plaster has been mixed in a plastic bowl, the bowl may be wiped clean with a damp paper towel or the plaster may be allowed to harden, after which gentle squeezing of the bowl will dislodge all of the plaster, which then can be dumped into a newspaper to be disposed of.

Plate 3. Drying rack. The unpainted frame for a New Orleans-type shutter (purchased from a lumber-hardware center) 28″ x 8″ x ¾″ was used. Half-inch dowels were cut 8½″ long. Half-inch holes were bored into the shutter frame. The dowels were then hammered into the holes (no nails or glue needed), and you have the perfect drying rack. When you get into production, you can make longer ones.

DRYING CASTINGS

Sand castings should be allowed to dry (in sunlight if possible) resting on blocks of wood or propped up in some manner so that air can circulate around them. It takes at least a week for a casting to "cure"—that is, reach maximum strength.

LACQUER

Must a sand casting, when it is thoroughly dry, be sprayed with lacquer? No, not always, but it helps. Lacquer makes the sand adhere more firmly and helps to anchor any shells or driftwood embedded in the castings. And, as we shall see later, when colored sands are used, several coats of lacquer are a must. On the other hand, the *Fish with a Nose for News* (made for editor, writer, and now director of college relations at Broward Community College. Edee Greene) has hung on an outside wall exposed to sun, wind, and rain for twenty years without suffering any deterioration—and it was not lacquered.

A casting should not be lacquered until it has had time to cure thoroughly.

Plate 4. *Fish with a Nose for News.* Made for Edee Greene, writer, editor, educator.

PHOTO SERIES   5   *Designing With Rope*

1. A small bowl is used to press into the sand.

2. Additional concentric circles were made with various-sized jar tops. A short piece of rope is pressed into the design.

3. Background of the design is textured with the handle of a plastic fork. The center of the design is a thumbprint. In the background is a small spray bottle for moistening the sand.

4. Another design is made by pressing a short section of rope into the sand in different positions.

5. The two completed castings.

PHOTO SERIES   6   *An "Ancient" Bas-Relief*

1. A sandbox has been prepared, the sand has been smoothed and dampened, and a shallow depression has been made by pressing with the hands. A drawing was made using a felt marker on a thin sheet of paper. (Note: Such sketches can be made on newspaper as well—use the classified or financial section.) The handle of a plastic fork is used to press the design into the sand.

2. Peeling the paper off.

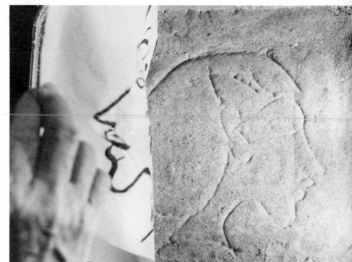

3. Refining and deepening the lines of the design. Water was splashed all over the design to form tiny craters.

4. For a small casting like this one, plaster can be mixed in an empty 24-oz. cottage cheese container. Plaster is carefully spooned onto the design.

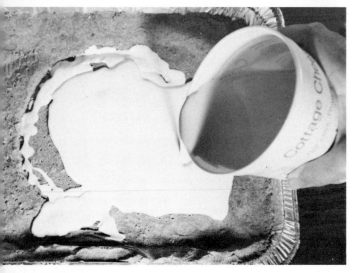

5. More plaster is poured.

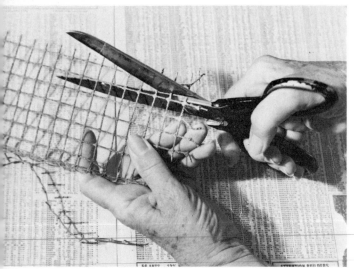

6. For reinforcement, a strip is cut from a scrap piece of plasterer's mesh.

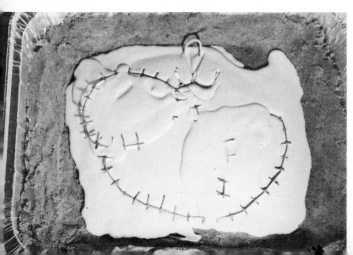

7. The strip of reinforcing wire has been inserted. A bit of armature wire has been looped to make a hanger, which is inserted into the freshly poured plaster. After this, the remainder of the plaster has been poured.

8. The completed casting. Note the texture made by the water splashes.

PHOTO SERIES 7 *Celestial Whirlpool*

1. The sandbox has been pre-pared. A rectangular depression has been made with a block of wood, after which the sides of the depression have been compacted by being pressed with the fingers. A design has been started using the modeling tool shown at right. A plastic spray bottle is used to moisten the sand so that lines made with the fork will be neat and will not crumble.

2. Some of the lines are made with the fork and now the design is being carried further with a modeling tool.

3. More modeling with the plastic fork.

4. Edges of the design are compacted and refined with a modeling tool and the fingers. After this a piece of shell will be inserted at the eye of the whirlpool.

5. Plaster was mixed in a plastic bowl. (For this piece we used 4 cups of water and about 6 cups of plaster.) A plastic spoon is used to fill the delicate details of the design.

6. Pouring plaster into the plastic spoon so that it will overflow gently.

7. Pouring the remainder of the plaster after picture wire was inserted to form a hanging loop.

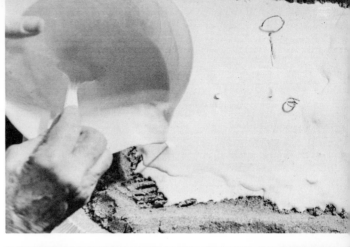

8. The plaster has set and hardened. The piece has been lifted out and turned over. Now excess sand is brushed off.

9. The completed casting hanging in a garden.

Plate 5a, b, and c. Three sunny faces.

Sand Castings Made From Pre- Modeled Forms 3

In this chapter we shall cut or model shapes out of various kinds of clay and press them into sand to make castings.

PHOTO SERIES 8 *A House Number*

1. A lump of clay is rolled into a flat layer with a rolling pin. Strips of wood are used as guides so that the clay will have an even thickness of ¾". Numerals have been cut from thin cardboard. The clay used here is a type of self-hardening clay bought from a hobby shop, but any potter's clay would work just as well.

2. The number 3 has been cut out and the artist is cutting the number 5. (The artist is using a potter's knife, but a paring knife could be used.) Care must be taken not to spoil the shape of the cut-out letters. The clay is still plastic and must be handled gently. (The cutting must be perpendicular—straight up and down.)

3. The edges of the numerals must be smoothed and made perfectly vertical. The handle of the potter's knife is used for this purpose.

4. A bed of sand has been prepared, tamped, smoothed, and made level. A spirit level is used to check the evenness of the surface. Strips of wood are used to press a border.

5. The numerals have dried in the sun for a day. (The clay could have been hardened by firing in a kiln, but that would have involved more time and extra expense.) The numerals are laid in place on the damp sand (backwards, of course!).

6. Pressing the numbers into the sand. The artist uses a block of wood and presses firmly so that each number goes into the sand to a depth of ½".

7. The sand will crack and push up a bit in places. Here, the artist is pressing sand against the numbers and carefully smoothing away the cracks in the sand.

8. Lifting out the numbers. They have broken under pressure, but that actually is an advantage because it makes them easier to remove without disturbing the pressing, and even though broken, the numbers can be reused for future castings. If a bit of sand is dislodged, use your fingers or a modeling tool to press it back in place.

9. Ready to pour. Two pieces of plastic drinking straws have been inserted to provide holes in the casting that will be used to fasten it to a wall.

10. Pouring.

11. Signing and dating the plaque while the plaster is still soft—five to ten minutes after pouring is completed.

12. The plaque is removed from the sand forty minutes later and washed with a hose. (Leaving the plaque in the sand longer won't hurt—in fact it is an advantage to let a piece this size harden a longer time.) The artist uses a stiff paintbrush to help in removing excess sand. (As soon as the washing was completed, the artist used a paring knife to scrape sand away from the top surfaces of the numerals so that the numbers would stand out in contrast to the background.)

13. The finished plaque. (Note: Great care must be used when the plaque is placed on a wall. Use small washers to act as a cushion, and don't screw the screws in too tightly or the plaque will crack. Be sure to let the plaque *cure* (harden) for a week or so before placing it.

PHOTO SERIES 9 *A Plaque Made From A Clay Form*

1. A stylized lion was modeled in clay and allowed to become bone dry.

2. The clay shape has been pressed into moist sand. The sand around the edge of the figure has been compacted by pressing firmly with the fingers and a modeling tool. The clay model has broken in several places, but that doesn't matter a bit. Wooden strips are used to form the rectangular frame of the plaque. Important note: Parts of the lion must touch the frame.

3. The clay lion is removed carefully; then the artist starts pouring plaster.

4. Continuing to pour plaster.

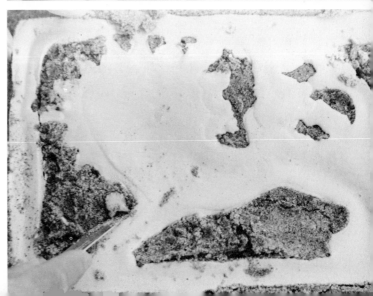

5. Trimming the edges of the design while the edges are still soft.

6. The finished plaque. Plaques of this sort fit well into room divider fixtures or into patio walls.

Some sandcrafters make models out of a mixture of flour, water, and salt. This unleavened dough (called *baker's clay*) baked in an oven and then varnished becomes hard enough to serve as a model to be pressed into the sand to make a casting.

Let's explore the use of baker's clay. To begin with, we will be making small objects to press into larger forms, such as eyes, nose, mouth, and various sizes and shapes of rays for sun faces. Of course, when you get the knack of sand casting and want to produce several of the same designs, you will then get into making complete designs in the baker's clay like the gingerbread man of old.

Recipe for *baker's clay:*

2 cups of flour (ordinary flour without yeast)
½ cup of salt
¾ cup of water

Mix the salt and flour, then add the water slowly as you mix or "cut" it with a fork the way Mother used to make pie dough. Keep pressing and mixing with the fork until all the flaky particles stick together and you can make a ball of dough in your hands.

Extra baker's clay may be stored in a plastic bag in the refrigerator to be used another day. However, it is best to use it rather promptly as it isn't like edible dough. Be sure to keep the finished pieces away from children—varnished *baker's clay is NOT EDIBLE.*

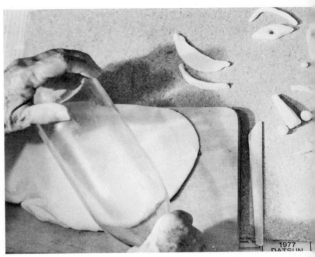

1. Knead the dough on a board. If it seems sticky, shake a little flour onto the board. Pinch, pull, flatten, and fold the dough over and over. Use the heel of your hand, pressing it forward into the dough as is being done here. Repeat this kneading until the ball of clay dough is soft and smooth as skin—at least fifteen minutes.

2. The forms at the right were rolled and cut or pinched into desired shapes. Now the artist is rolling the dough with a bottle. (If the dough sticks to the bottle, dust a little flour on the surface of the dough.)

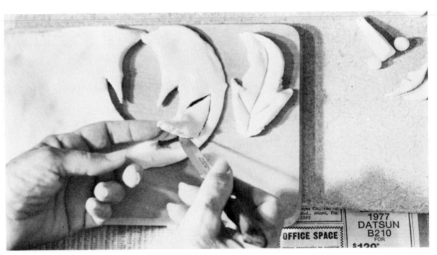

3. Leaf forms and triangular shapes are cut, scored, and twisted. (Use a modeling tool or paring knife.) After you have made the shapes you need, place them on a cookie sheet or double layer of aluminum foil. Put them in the oven at about 300°F. In a half hour check the thinner pieces for hardness. If they are baked to complete hardness, remove, leaving larger, thicker pieces to continue baking. It won't hurt if they get brown—but don't let them burn.

When the pieces have cooled, remove them from the cookie sheet, place them on foil or newspaper in an open place, and spray them with polyurethane varnish. (This varnish dries quickly, but if you spray the second and third coats on before the preceding coat is hard dry, the pieces will be sticky.) Spray both sides of each piece until they are thoroughly coated. Note: When baker's clay pieces are not in use, store them in airtight boxes or plastic bags because high humidity will soften them.

PHOTO SERIES   11   *Making A Sunface With Pressings Of Baker's Clay Shapes*

1. With a spoon, an oval shape is scooped out in moist sand. The sand is packed into a gentle curve at the edge, using the fingers or a spoon as shown here.

2. Using the baker's clay shapes, the artist has pressed features in to make the face. Lips and brow pieces are seen in the upper left, nose and eye pieces in the upper right. A shell is used to press cheeks. The pieces to be used as the sun's rays are ready to be pressed in.

3. The various ray shapes are alternated around the oval. These must be pressed deeply so that they won't be too fragile in the final piece.

4. Plaster has been poured. Reinforcements cut from a scrap of plasterer's wire mesh have been put in place. A wire hanger is centered near the top. The final plaster is being poured.

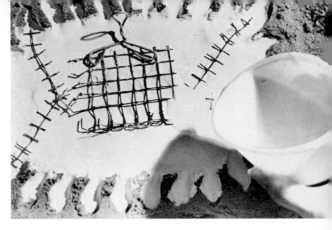

5. The finished piece on an outside wall. It has been sprayed with several coats of polyurethane mat varnish.

Plate 6. Sunface made with pressings of baker's clay.

Free-Standing Sculpture 4

U p to now, everything we have made was intended to be hung on a wall. Now we shall learn how to sandcast a piece of sculpture to be mounted on a pedestal.

PHOTO SERIES   12   *A Sculptured Head*

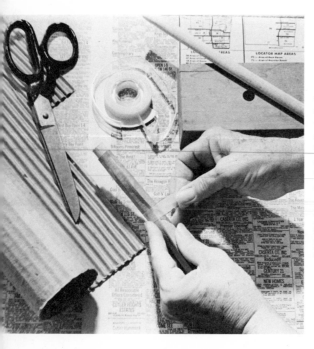

1. We have a block of wood with a ½″ diameter hole bored in it which will hold a section of ½″ dowel to support the finished sculpture. The artist is wrapping another section of ½″ dowel with a layer of corrugated paper. This is being fastened with Scotch tape and will then be covered with sandwich wrap. This second piece of dowel will be placed in the neck of the sculpture when the plaster is poured. The extra wrapping will make it possible to pull the dowel out of the form after the plaster has set. The wood will be pulled out first and the paper wrapping will then be removed easily.

2. Sand has been moistened thoroughly and pushed up to form an oblong mound. A bowl is scooped out to form a hollow for the head with an elongated neck scooped out too. Here, features are being pressed in with a modeling tool.

3. Modeling of features is complete. The sand sculpture is sprayed with water. Notice how the pile of sand has been compacted by hand all around to contain the sculpture. When you spray, be sure to spray the entire mound so that it won't collapse when you pour the plaster.

4. Plaster has been mixed to the right creamy consistency and with a small spoon is being carefully poured into the features. (Note the wrapped ½″ dowel in the background.)

5. A small plastic cheese box was dipped into the bowl of plaster. Plaster is being poured into the small plastic spoon to allow it to spill over into the head. Gentle pouring is most important here because the delicate drawing of the features could be ruined if the force of the pouring is too heavy.

6. Now plaster is spooned onto the upper edge of the hollowed out head. The plaster runs down to the middle leaving a wall of plaster.

7. The running of the plaster on the walls is continued. The plaster will naturally run to the center, but the sculpture would be top heavy if it were solid. Be sure to give the sides several coats of plaster—always from the top of the sides.

8. Then, with the spoon excess plaster is scooped out from the middle of the neck and head and splashed against the sides to thicken them. Don't leave any thin spots in the wall.

9. The ½″ dowel in the background of the preceding pictures is being placed. It must stick out at both ends. Do not press it too hard, but be sure it is firmly set in the center of the neck.

10. Plaster is poured over the dowel. Pour carefully and be sure to build it up sufficiently by going back and forth over that area as you pour.

11. The plaster is now in the cream cheese state and can be modeled. With the bowl of the spoon the plaster is being pushed up onto the sides to make them thicker. DON'T PRESS—just let the spoon glide as it pushes the plaster around. If you press you may dislodge the plaster from the sand.

12. The sculpture was allowed to dry for two hours; then it was removed from the sand, washed, and irregular edges scraped. After this it was allowed to harden for three days. The dowel was pulled out and the paper wrapping was removed. Now the standing dowel is in the wooden block and the head is in position.

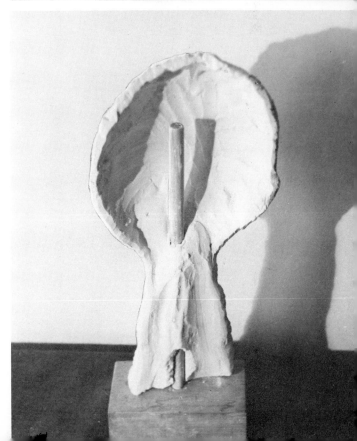

13. The completed sculpture.

PHOTO SERIES 13 *Farm Couple, Two Free-Standing Figurines*

1. Farmer and his wife were modeled in clay and allowed to harden. A piece of coat-hanger wire was used as an armature in each figurine. The separate parts were not attached to make pressing them into the sand easier.

2. The female figure has been pressed into the sand. In this case the sand was not too firmly compacted so that the figure could easily be pushed into it. The fingers and a thin piece of wood were used to compact the sand around the figure. A piece of glass has been pressed into the sand to permit building up plaster at the base of the figurine. Note: When glass is placed in the sand against which plaster will be built up for a footing, be sure the glass is absolutely straight, or, better still, leaning at a very slight angle, toward the piece. This will keep the piece in balance when it is standing free.

3. The clay forms are carefully removed, features are pressed in with a pointed modeling tool, and the other modeling tools are used where needed to refine the pressing. Notice that the skirt has been extended until it touches the glass. Modeling tools are used to make ruffled pleats. Pieces of armature wire are cut and shaped to fit areas needing reinforcement—arms and neck. (Armature wire is made of soft aluminum.)

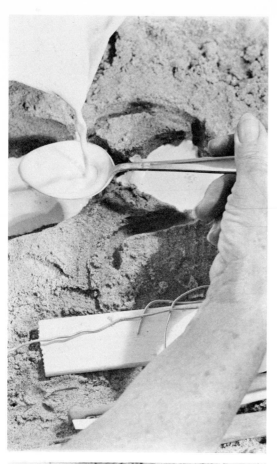

4. Beginning to pour plaster.

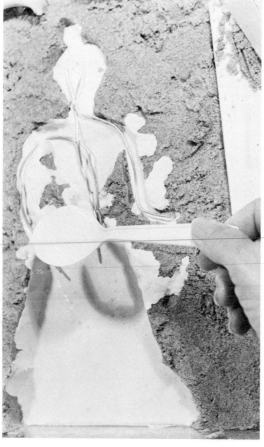

5. Armature wire in place; plaster is carefully spooned to cover the wire.

6. Toward the end of the pouring process the plaster will start to thicken. Plaster which has reached the cheese state was used to build a base against the glass. Here, the edge of the figurine is trimmed with a wooden modeling tool. (The thin flat edge is used. A small paring knife could be used.)

Before you remove the piece from the sand after it has thoroughly dried (an hour of drying would be wise in this case because of the thickness of plaster in parts of the pouring), take the glass by the edges in two hands and gently move it from side to side and then up and out. Glass releases smoothly and easily from the fresh plaster. Do not force it out!

The farmer was made the same way as his wife.

7. The couple standing on a backyard fence.

Plate 7a and b. Two Amazons in a garden. The bases of these figurines were made as described in Photo Series 13.

PHOTO SERIES 14   *A Fish With A Glass Eye*

1. The form of a fish has been scooped out of the sand. At the bottom, note that a piece of wood covered with plastic (sandwich wrap) has been inserted edgewise at the base of the figure.

2. The opening of the eye was marked with a small bottle top and then was dug out of the sand. A cylinder about an inch in diameter and 2½″ tall was shaped out of clay, allowed to harden, and then wrapped with Scotch tape. (The tape makes removal from the hardened plaster much easier.) This cylinder is being inserted where we wish to have an opening in the sculpture. (Note: Any small cylindrical shape could serve as well as one made of clay, but be sure to wrap it with Scotch tape.)

3. Spooning plaster into the impression. At the upper right we see a wire coat hanger bent into shape to serve as reinforcement. Also notice the space around the cylinder—that is made so that plaster will make a protrusion in the sand upon which the glass eye will be glued when the plaster is thoroughly dry.

4. Pouring partially completed. Floor of the design is covered with plaster, and the coat-hanger wire has been put in place.

5. The remainder of the plaster has been poured. A small portion of the plaster was poured into a separate cup to slake while the fish design was being covered with plaster. This was stirred until it started to thicken, and then a base for the fish was built up by spooning plaster against the plastic covered stick, as shown in Photo Series 13.

6. The completed sculpture. The eye is made out of a glass button (a flattened glass marble) of the type sold in craft shops. The pupil of the eye was painted on the back of the glass with acrylic paint. The edge of the protrusion was scraped with a paring knife to remove sand and to make a flat resting place for the glass eye. (This must be done within two days, since after that the plaster will set too hard to do it easily.) The eye may then be glued in place in six or seven days. The plaster must be thoroughly dry before any gluing is done. (Use a synthetic white glue or china/glass glue.) This piece of sculpture is effective and decorative when a small light fixture is placed behind it.

Open Sculptural Forms 5

PHOTO SERIES 15   *See-Through Fish*

1. Again we use a fish motif. This piece of sculpture is too big for an aluminum pan, so we must use our executive sandbox. The shape of the fish has been scooped out. Islands of firmly compacted sand have been made. A seashell has been inserted to form an eye. Two more seashells were pushed into the sand at the top of the fish and another under the central island. (Leave only enough within the intaglio design so that the plaster will hold the shells fast.) A short piece of rope (shown upper left) was pressed into the sand to form the fish's gill. Scales and stripes in the design were made with wooden modeling tools. A piece of picture wire (top center) has been shaped to form a hanger. Plaster is being spooned into the design.

2. Continuing to spoon plaster into the design. Reinforcing wires have been laid in place.

53

3. Completing the pouring. Plaster is poured from the bowl into the spoon and allowed to flow gently over the entire shape. The two islands are not covered.

4. The plaster is set, and the sculpture is being brushed off with a whisk broom. Then the piece is thoroughly washed. You will find that at this stage there will be some refining to do—cleaning edges, making openings a bit wider, etc. But remember, handle your piece with care as the plaster is quite damp and fragile at this point.

5. The completed open sculptural form shown with a second fish made the same way.

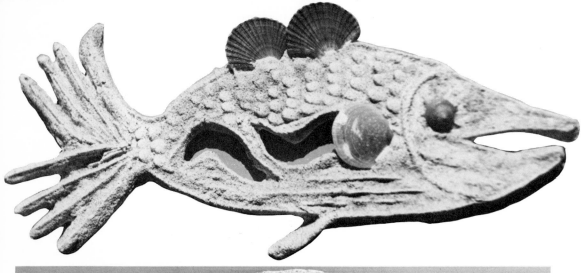

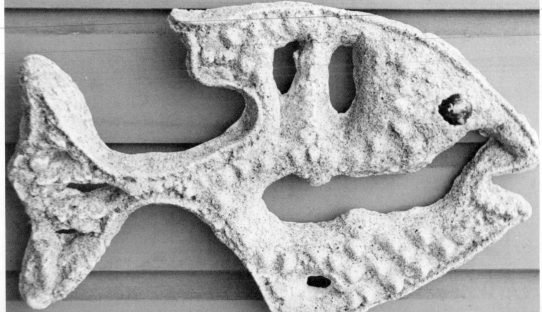

Hollow Casting

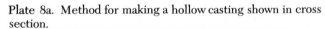

ow would you like to test your ingenuity? Now that you have learned how to design in reverse (intaglio) in sand, why not try hollow sculpture—designing in the round. (In sand casting such designs are done not only reverse, but also upside down.)

In order to explain how to make a hollow casting in sand, it seemed a good idea to do a cut-away in a 2-qt. clear plastic container. The cut-away is only so that you can see the basic way to hollow cast in sand. When you actually do a casting in a large bowl or a bucket, you can only look in at the top and what finally comes out will be a surprise.

Plate 8a. Method for making a hollow casting shown in cross section.

This photo shows how the moist sand (it must be moist throughout) is compacted in a container. The tumbler in the background was used to make the hollow form. The drinking straws are cut and inserted to show how you can insert rolled cardboard shapes, shells, etc., into the compacted wall of sand.

Anything like straws or rolled forms must be hollow so that they can "eat" the sand rather than dislodge it, which could crack the carefully packed wall. (You will see later that flatter objects such as shells may be pressed in gently or carefully pushed in to protrude in the final piece.)

The cup in the foreground could be a cheese cup, an ice cream cup—anything that fits into the hollow loosely enough to leave at least ¼" to ⅜" of space around it for pouring plaster. The straw at the base shows the depth the plaster must be before the smaller cup is inserted into the cavity. The sand in the smaller cup is there as a weight to hold the cup in place in the wet plaster—just enough to keep it from floating out of place when you pour the rest of the plaster in.

Here you can see how the smaller cup goes in and how the pieces you insert as projections in the final design must leave room for the cup. If you intend to have holes for light in your piece, the projections must just barely touch the cup. You'll see why in the next photo series.

Plate 8b. Method for making a hollow casting shown in cross section.

PHOTO SERIES   16   *A Jewel Of A Night Light*

While we have our 2-qt. freezer container handy, let's make an upside-down hollow casting.

1. Moist sand is pressed firmly into the container (the hollow form, the plastic tumbler, is in the center resting on about 2" or 3" of sand). Be sure the sand is thoroughly moist throughout so there will be no shifting or crumbling of the shell of sand when you remove the tumbler. The smaller cup at right is loosely wrapped in sandwich wrap.

2. The tumbler is gently twisted out. (The sand you see in the tumbler is just extra sand that was not needed in the tamping down process.)

3. Here various-sized cylinders are made of flexible cardboard (from a cereal box in this case). The cylinders are covered with Scotch tape and in some cases have been deliberately distorted. The tumbler in the background is holding cut pieces of plastic drinking straws. The plastic fork (front left) has been used to make a texture in the walls of the casting.

4. The hollow uncovered ends of the small cylinders are pressed into the sand. Since the plan is to have light come through our hollow casting, the forms are pressed in just enough so that the inner cup will touch the Scotch-tape covered ends and plaster will not seal the intended holes.

5. The straws and cylinders are now all in place. (Notice the fluted edging made by pressing in the tines of the larger fork seen in the preceding photo.) Here the artist is pouring the floor of the cavity. (The floor becomes the top in the final casting—so pour only to the edge of the cylinders inserted in the bottom of the cavity.)

6. The sandwich-wrap-covered cup is now placed gently onto the freshly poured plaster "floor." Plaster is dipped out of the larger bowl into a small plastic cheese cup, then poured around the sides to form the wall of our hollow casting.

7. Here more plaster is being poured around the top edge. As the plaster settles, it will leave a slight depression, as seen in the top of the pouring—this must be filled or the base of your casting will be fragile and might crumble.

8. The artist uses a paring knife to cut away the spillover. This is done after the plaster has settled for five minutes or a little more.

9. The poured piece is allowed to stand for at least an hour before the cup is removed. (Handling a piece of this shape too soon after pouring could make it collapse.) Here you see the advantage of a plastic cup—you can pull the edges toward the center and then twist as you lift out. Remove the sandwich wrap next and let the piece stand for another fifteen or twenty minutes.

10. Now lift the container and let the sand casting mold slide out of the container.

11. Carefully crumble the sand away from the casting. This piece is small enough to rinse off in your clean-up pail of water.

12. With a paring knife, poke into each cavity; if a film of plaster has collected inside, it is easy to ream it out at this point. All of the projections—straws and cylinders—are carefully removed and the piece is washed once again. Notice how the rim of one of the openings has been scraped. That is done at each opening where you might wish to place a glass button or flattened glass marble. The rim is scraped so that the glass will set in snugly. When the piece has thoroughly dried for several days, glue the glass buttons into place with a good bonding glue that dries crystal clear.

13. The finished piece (shown also in color).

PHOTO SERIES   17   *A Bit Of Clowning*

Now that you have tried one hollow casting, why not try another! This one will be a head, and since we cannot be too sure how the face will turn out, let's be frank and call it a clown—that way, whatever comes out will be fun. All steps are basically the same as in Photo Series 16.

1. Here we are putting sand from the beach into a 5-qt. bucket. First, sand is compacted to make a firm flooring. (Remember to keep the sand moist!) The spray bottle of water is at hand in the background and a small piece of wood for tamping in areas where it is difficult to use the fingers.

2. A 64-oz. soft drink bottle is set in the middle of the bucket and rests on the sandy floor that was just finished. Now the artist has filled in the space around the bottle and is tamping it down. The masking tape on the bottle is there as a guide so that when the sand is compacted up to that point, you will know that the top is even and that the piece will be as deep as you planned (deep enough so that it will sit easily over a small electric light unit—at least 4″ outside and 3½″ or so inside).

3. The artist twists the bottle slowly as it is pulled out of the well-tamped bed of sand. The sand is then sprayed with water and the features—a curved fragment of shell for the nose, two snail shells for eyes—are inserted. Ears are pressed in with the fingers, hair pressed with the flat edge of a modeling tool, or the tines of a fork. Now, remember—all of this is upside down as your work; the top is now the bottom and the bottom is the top. All shells must be pressed so that parts will be imbedded in the poured plaster. Cut pieces of drinking straws will be pressed in above and below the eyes. A shell fragment for buck teeth is inserted, and—to make the problem really tough—a shell that looks like a cigar will be placed in a corner of the clown's mouth.

4. Plaster is being spooned onto the floor of the depression. Notice the straws projecting into the cavity; these will make the holes for light to filter through. The two over the eyes are a guide to how much plaster to pour in this step. Don't let plaster flow over the tops of the straws because it will close the holes.

5. Now the cheese cup with sand is being held in the center of the depression. It is resting on the plaster that was just spooned in.

6. The plaster pouring has been completed, the bowls and spoons cleaned in the clean-up pail, and now the time is right to cut away excess plaster around the rim of the casting. The top of the cheese box is the guide for cutting an even flat edge.

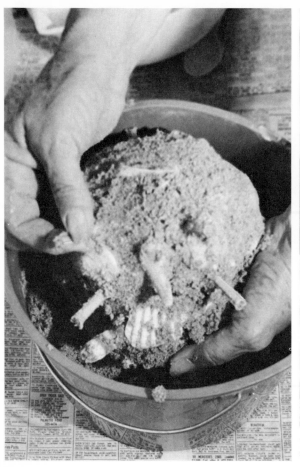

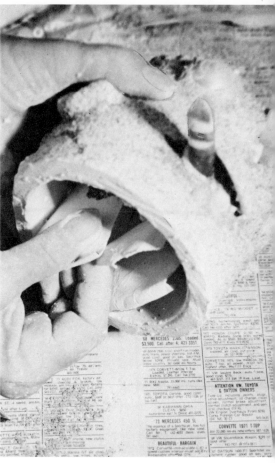

7. The piece has hardened for two hours. Here it is lifted out of the sand, and the straws are removed. The head is ready to wash.

8. This plastic cheese box was not wrapped with sandwich wrap, so in order to remove it, it is pulled toward the center, cut in strips, and pulled out.

9. The finished piece. Acrylic colors were used to paint the clown's mouth and eyes after the sand had been scraped away. When the clown is lighted the black marks become little arrows of light, thus making a fun kind of light.

The owl was made the same way as the clown and the jeweled light. The eyes were formed by inserting small cylinders of light cardboard covered with Scotch tape into the walls of the depression with the open ends embedded in the sand. The ears are small red ripple shells and the beak a curved fragment of shell. The feather impressions were made by random pressing of the handle of a plastic spoon.

Here is the owl sitting on a block of wood; he can be wired as a night light. Our owl is a howling success!

Plate 8c. Owl's head.

Color 7

*S*o far the only color in our work (except for the fish's glass eye) has come from sand and shells. Now we shall use colored sand purchased from a craft shop.

PHOTO SERIES   18   *An Open Circular Plaque Using Colored Sand*

1. Regular sand is compacted as firmly as possible with a heavy block of wood.

2. A large skillet cover is used to press a circle in the sand. A wood modeling tool is used to form a trough around the lid. (If you prefer, you can make a circle out of cardboard or paper and draw around it with a wooden modeling tool.)

3. Beginning to draw a design—a rooster motif.

4. The drawing is completed in the sand and scooped out.

5. Adding color. Bags of colored sand have been purchased from a craft store (they come in ½-lb. and 1-lb. bags). Here yellow sand is spooned into the area of the rooster's bill. Clean the tiny plastic spoon after each color has been spooned on; otherwise you will "dirty" the sands. (Keep a dry paper towel handy for this—don't use water, as you want the spoon dry.)

6. More sands of different colors are spooned into the proper areas.

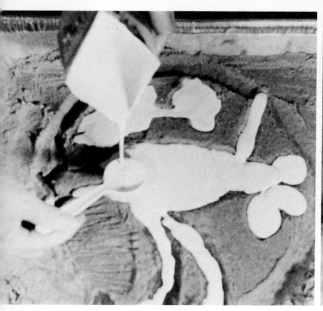

7. Pouring plaster using a cut-down milk carton and a plastic spoon.

8. The pouring completed. While the plaster is still soft, a knife is used to trim the edges of the design. (Remember, the piece will be quite fragile for a few days—so when the plaster is set and the piece is washed, you will be doing quite a bit of refining of all edges. Try not to exert any pressure on the piece, but scrape gently to remove any excess plaster.)

9. The completed plaque (also shown in color).

As a final step, any sand casting in which colored sands have been used *must* be sprayed with several coats of lacquer. Note: When you remove the casting from the sand, you will notice a residue of colored sand in the sandbox. Just remove it by skimming it off the top of the casting sand with a spoon and dispose of it. There will be small particles of color left here and there—just moisten, mix, and get your sandbox ready for the next casting.

PHOTO SERIES 19 *Bas-Relief Using Colored Sand*

1. The sandbox has been prepared (this one is filled with fine white sand, which is best for delicate detail), a rectangular depression has been made, and the sand has been compacted by tamping with the block of wood. Here, figures of two dancing children are modeled in intaglio with modeling tools and fingers. The round heads are impressions made by pressing bottle tops in the sand.

    After this, colored sand (bags shown at left) is applied. In the photo center (lower edge) the artist is dusting colored sand into the casting. A very small plastic spoon or the handle of a plastic utensil is good for this. Once all color has been placed in the design, the impression is sprinkled with water and the plaster is poured.

    As in the preceding photo series, the plaster is first spooned into the intricate areas, then poured into the bowl of a larger spoon to allow the plaster to flow gently over the entire depression; a wire loop for hanging is placed just before the last of the plaster is poured.

    When the plaque dried for about a day, the areas of the faces, arms, and legs were scraped smooth (free of all sand) and modeled slightly with a small thin modeling tool. (As you scrape you will notice how wet the plaster is—so use a delicate touch! Take care not to remove nose, eyes, and lips.)

    Now you are ready to paint the scraped areas with acrylic colors. First, brush the scraped areas with acrylic medium to prepare the plaster for color. Then mix flesh tones of acrylic colors; paint on features as soon as flesh tones have dried.

    Let the plaque dry for a week, then give it several coats of acrylic spray varnish.

2. The final plaque (also shown in color).

The plaque we just made could have been poured in a frame, provided nails were partially but securely driven into the inner surface of the frame to anchor the casting in place, as shown in plates 9 and 10.

Two sand castings poured in frames are shown in color plates.

Plate 9. Frame.   Plate 10. Frame.

PHOTO SERIES 20 *A Plaque Using Colored Sand And A Design Wheel*

1. The design strip impressed at the left was made with a design wheel (as shown in photo—it is seen to the right by modeling tools). The birds were scooped out and selected shells pressed into the design. (If you can't collect shells at a beach, you may buy small boxes of shells from craft stores.) A twig was pressed to make the tree form. The modeling tools were used to refine and compact edges of the impressions. Constant spraying to keep the sand properly moist is extremely important here. Colored sands were sprinkled on the design, then plaster was carefully poured.

2. Finished design, lacquered and hanging on a wall (also shown in color).

Stained Glass 8

    reating with stained glass is a special craft which requires a lot of study before an artist becomes proficient. But we can obtain beautiful effects quite easily by combining pieces of stained glass with our castings. All we need to know is where to obtain stained glass (see section on sources of supply) and how to cut it into desired shapes.

PHOTO SERIES 21 *Cutting Glass*

1. You will need a glass cutter with a hard steel wheel and a ball at the end of the handle. Clean the glass with liquid glass cleaner. Put several layers of newspaper on the table and place the glass on the newspaper—smoother side up. Hold the glass cutter vertically between thumb and first finger. Exerting pressure, make a firm continuous even stroke without pausing or lifting the cutter.

2. Tap the underside of the scored line with the ball end of the glass cutter until you see a fracture developing under the scored line.

3. Use two hands to snap the two pieces of glass apart.

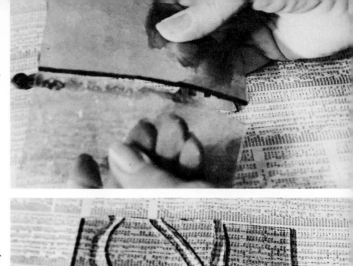

4. Small rounded shapes can be cut from a larger piece of glass by making a series of short curved strokes with the glass cutter.

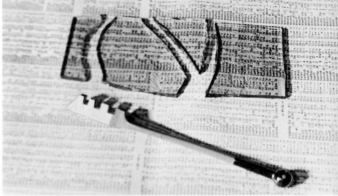

5. To cut straight edges, you will need a ruler to guide the cutter. The problem here is that it is almost impossible to keep the ruler from slipping as you cut. A strip of two-sided masking tape stuck to the underside of the ruler will hold it in place. (Note: After you have made your cut, put the ruler aside, *tape side up*—it will stick to anything! When you are all through cutting, the tape can be peeled off the ruler.)

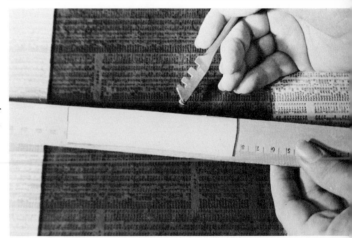

6. After a straight cut has been made, place the piece of glass on the tabletop with the scored line just barely beyond the edge of the table and parallel to it. Press the glass down on the table with one hand; use the other hand to press the glass downward.

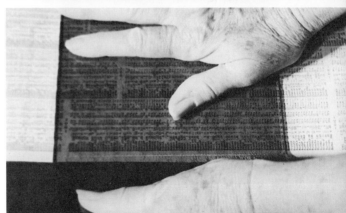

7. It should snap with a clean line.

Don't be discouraged by failure on your first try; the glass-cutting process is simple and with a little practice you will develop skill. (Save your "failures"; you'll create designs in which they may be used.)

Glass craftsmen are concerned about the neatness of the edges of their cuts—rough edges or little projections interfere with their designs. Since, in our work, all the glass edges are embedded in plaster or glue, such roughness or tiny projections need not bother us unduly.

SAFETY PRECAUTIONS

Glass can cut—and cuts are painful. Glass slivers getting in the skin are worse. Take care in handling glass. Avoid having cut edges come in contact with your fingers. Work on newspaper so that the glass slivers can be folded into the newspaper and discarded.

PHOTO SERIES   22   *A Colorful Geometric Plaque*

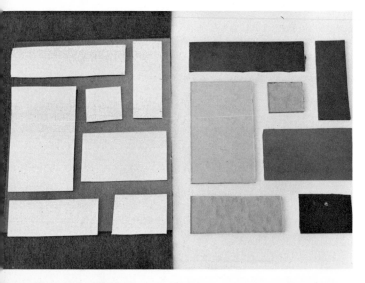

1. A design was planned by cutting rectangles of paper and arranging them in various positions. When a design deemed satisfactory was obtained (left), pieces of stained glass were cut to the same sizes as the paper patterns.

2. The sandbox has been prepared with white mason sand or silica sand. (This sand is almost pure white and is extra fine.) An area for our design has been tamped as firmly as possible and made absolutely level (we shall see later why this is important). A spirit level on top of our tamping block shows us that our design bed is truly level. Keep the water spray bottle handy, as this sand must be kept moist.

3. The tamping block is moved around to make a rectangled depression the size of our planned plaque.

4. The pieces of glass are laid in position as a final check on the design. At the upper left corner are two strips of wood which will be used to press depressions into the bed of sand—

5. —like this.

6. The depressions have been made with the strips of wood.

7. Pouring plaster. (If the sand were not level the plaster would not flow evenly.)

8. Inserting strips of picture wire for reinforcement and to provide hanging loops—one on each side. (Make loops small enough so that they won't be visible when the plaque is finally hanging on a wall or at a window.)

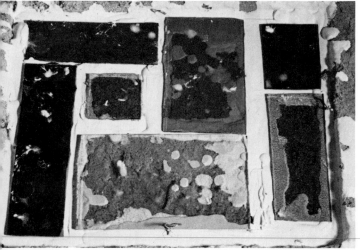

9. The reinforcing wires have been covered and plaster has been poured to fill all of the depressions. Now the pieces of stained glass have been laid on the sand platforms overlapping the wet plaster.

10. More plaster has been poured to cover all of the edges of the pieces of glass. The fact that the plaster has spilled over the glass is unimportant, as it can be easily chipped and cleaned off. Note the four hanging loops—one on each side projecting from the plaster.

After this step, the plaster was allowed to stand for thirty minutes, by which time it was quite cool to the touch; then a wooden modeling tool was used to remove all of the plaster that had spilled over the glass. Care must be taken not to put pressure on any part of the design. (The plaster will need a week to cure—to be thoroughly hard-dry.)

Next, the piece was removed from the sand and washed; then excess bits of plaster were removed from the front of the design. (You will find that very little plaster has run onto the glass in front, but remove it while it is still fresh.)

11. The completed plaque (shown also in color).

Let's try another method of incorporating stained glass into a sand casting. This time we shall use glass scraps and two circular shapes (bought from a hobby shop). We shall use a method of sandwiching the glass shapes between layers of clay.

PHOTO SERIES 23   *Glass Sandwiches*

A depression was made in a sandbox the size of our panel. The sand was tamped and leveled and the pieces of glass were arranged to form a design. When a satisfactory arrangement was arrived at, the pieces of glass were pressed gently into the sand to mark the placing of each piece.

1. A layer of clay is rolled out. A bottle is used as a rolling pin. Strips of wood ½" thick are used as guides for even thickness.

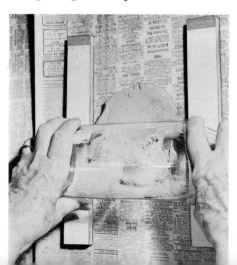

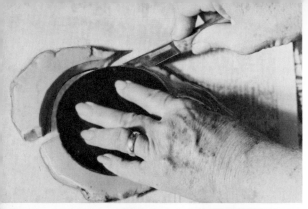

2. A circle is cut out of the ½″ slab of clay the exact size of the circle to be used.

3. After the clay was cut, ⅛″ was trimmed off all around the circle. Then another layer of clay was rolled—this time using strips of wood ⅛″ thick. The clay circle ½″ thick was laid on the second slab of clay with a small piece of newspaper in between; then a circle was cut from the thinner layer exactly the same size as the thicker circle of clay. Here we see the artist making a sandwich. In her left hand she holds the circle of glass; in her right hand is the ½″ circle of clay. Underneath on the table we see the ⅛″ circle of clay.

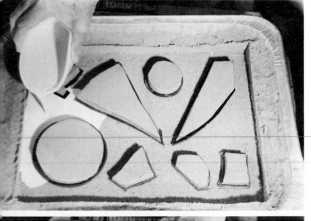

4. The artist holds the circular sandwich. The thicker layer of clay is on top, the thinner layer underneath. To the left are two scraps of glass which have been sandwiched between layers of clay in the same manner as the circle.

5. The sandwiches are all in place, thin layer down. Plaster is being poured.

6. Continuing to pour plaster.

7. Inserting a hanging wire. After this more plaster was poured to make the plaque the thickness of the sandwiches.

8. Forty minutes later, the plaster has set and cooled; the plaque has been lifted out of the sand and washed. The upper layers of the sandwiches (the thicker ones) are being lifted out with a paring knife. Any spillovers are trimmed off at this time.

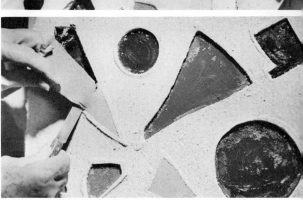

9. The plaque has been turned over; the thinner layers of clay are being lifted out of the front of the plaque. After all residue of plaster is trimmed away from the glass, a damp paper towel is used to clean the glass shapes.

10. The finished plaque. Note how the pressing of the pieces of glass into the sand at the beginning of the series produced an interesting border around each piece of glass. The plaque is also shown in color.

Another panel—a standing one, made by the method just described— is shown in color.

11. The plaque in sunlight.

1. Here is still another method of using stained glass. A portrait of a city street has been modeled in intaglio. This will be a free-standing form, so a piece of glass has been pressed edgewise into the sand. (The glass will have plaster built up against it to form the foot.) The trees could have been modeled freehand or twigs could have been used to create the tree shapes, but actually what was used here was a piece of seaweed, which proved to be the right shape and quite malleable. The leaves were formed by pressings made with the round end of a small modeling tool.

Openings for the stained glass were made in a manner similar to that used for the glass-eyed fish in Photo Series 14. Rectangular and round shapes were modeled in clay, allowed to harden, then wrapped with Scotch tape.

2. Modeling has been carried further, more openings have been provided, and pebbles have been inserted beneath the sidewalk at the foot of the tree.

After this step, plaster was poured over the design. More plaster was splashed against the glass and built up to make the foot. Because of its size it was allowed to harden for forty-five minutes; then the casting was removed and washed. During the washing the clay forms softened so that they were easy to remove.

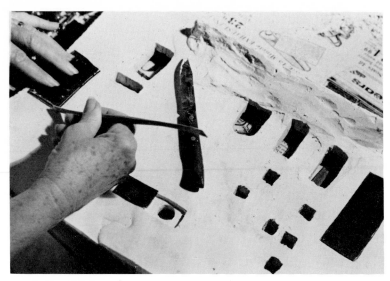

3. As soon as the casting had been washed and the clay shapes removed, openings were trimmed and smoothed with a paring knife. Here the flat end of a wooden modeling tool is being used to score the area around an opening to be recessed so that the piece of glass selected will fit in and be flush with the surface of the back. The piece of glass at the right is already in place. Another area in the center, by the hand, is ready to have the glass dropped in. When all of the areas were recessed, the glass was removed, and acrylic was sprayed on to seal the plaster. It was allowed to dry for several days, and then each piece was glued in place with a glue suitable for glass and plaster.

4. The finished cityscape. This photo shows the interesting textures. Note also that parts of the design were gently scraped to give contrast of sand and plaster (also shown in color).

Different Casting Materials 9

ﬂydrocal Gypsum Cement and Hydrostone Gypsum Cement, products of the U.S. Gypsum Company, are two forms of plaster of paris which set harder and stronger than molding plaster. (Hydrostone is the

Plate 11. Cement casting.

stronger of the two.) They are mixed in the same manner as molding plaster; they cost two to three times as much.

Fast-setting pouring cement for anchoring posts and filling holes in floors is sold in hardware stores and building-supply shops under a variety of trade names. Castings made with this material are much harder and much lighter than those made with molding plaster, but it costs a great deal more. You may be interested in trying pouring cement; it comes in 1-lb. and 5-lb. packages.

We have experimented with several different brands and have learned that no two work exactly the same way. We have also learned that it is best to disregard directions on the packages and just sprinkle 1 lb. of the material into a cupful of water and start stirring immediately. A little more cement or a little more water can be added if needed to make a smooth, creamy liquid that can be poured. Then pour at once.

This material sets very quickly, but don't disturb the pouring for twenty-four hours. A casting can be trimmed right after it has been poured and has begun to set, but it is impossible to do any trimming or scraping once the cement has set.

Our best results have been obtained with a light gray pouring cement, Por-Rok (see plate 11), and a white pouring cement, Gable-Tite White Cement (shown in color).

Builder's pre-mix cement is coming into favor with some sculptors who are beginning to make castings in sand for the embellishment of buildings and building lobbies as well as for large outdoor plaques.

SAFETY PRECAUTIONS

Danger—cement is a hazardous material! Read and follow safety precautions on the box.

Avoid getting cement in or near the eyes. Don't mix it in a windy area. Wash hands thoroughly after working with cement. Some craftsmen who work with this material recommend using rubber gloves.

Careers 10

Creators of beautiful objects sooner or later begin to think of selling their work. There are many outlets for the home-studio craftsman—church bazaars, hobby fairs, etc. Often, admiring friends buy pieces to give to their friends and so, by word of mouth, a clientele is built up.

But can one make a living, or even a partial living, from sand casting? The answer is yes, it can be done and some people are doing it, but the step from amateur to professional is a big one. To make a living, the craftsman must become a mass producer and this means a completely different life-style.

Let's visit *Sandcrafters*, a successful production studio operated by Betty Oram in her garage (the family car stays parked outdoors). Betty makes plaques. She is a gifted artist whose work has simplicity and great charm. Her style is her own—note how areas of her designs have been scraped free of sand to provide a subtle contrast between the white of the plaster and the sand color.

We asked her the nitty-gritty question—how does one make out financially? "Working alone, one can make only a partial living," she said, "yet making pieces for sale is worth the effort."

Betty works hard. She uses Hydrocal and usually pours four plaques at a time, rarely making more than six in a day. There is much physical work—lifting sand, plaster, the plaques themselves. (Evidently this work has kept her in great shape. We were amazed to learn that this gal with the figure and features of a woman in her mid-twenties is a grandmother!)

Betty says that to embark on a full-time commercial career one must employ at least one assistant, a sales representative, and an agent. Her pieces are sold by gift shops. She has all the orders she can fill. Although she reproduces her designs many times, no two are exactly alike because she does not use molds.

She plans, soon, to go into the production of larger pieces—plaques for gardens and for architectural decoration. We hope she does. We are happy with those examples of her work that we now own and we look forward to seeing how she will expand her horizons.

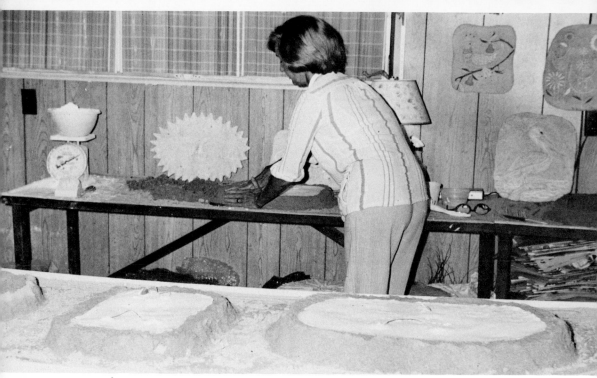

Plate 12. Betty Oram in her studio.

Plate 13. Plaques by Betty Oram.

Ideas And Explorations 11

*S*and casting goes on forever. Now that you have learned the techniques, you are ready to dream up ideas all your own.

A sketchbook helps. Keep one with you so that when something triggers an idea for a sand casting you can jot it down: an old building with a strange ornament over the door, a bird perched on a gnarled tree branch, a dried milkweed pod, an animal sleeping in his cage in the zoo, children at play, or just the idea of a special holiday or the way a few fish are displayed in the fish market—anything at all can send you home to do more sand castings. Hang loose and let ideas flow, but don't lose them—jot them down.

Here are some notes from the author's sketchbook.

Variety of sunbursts

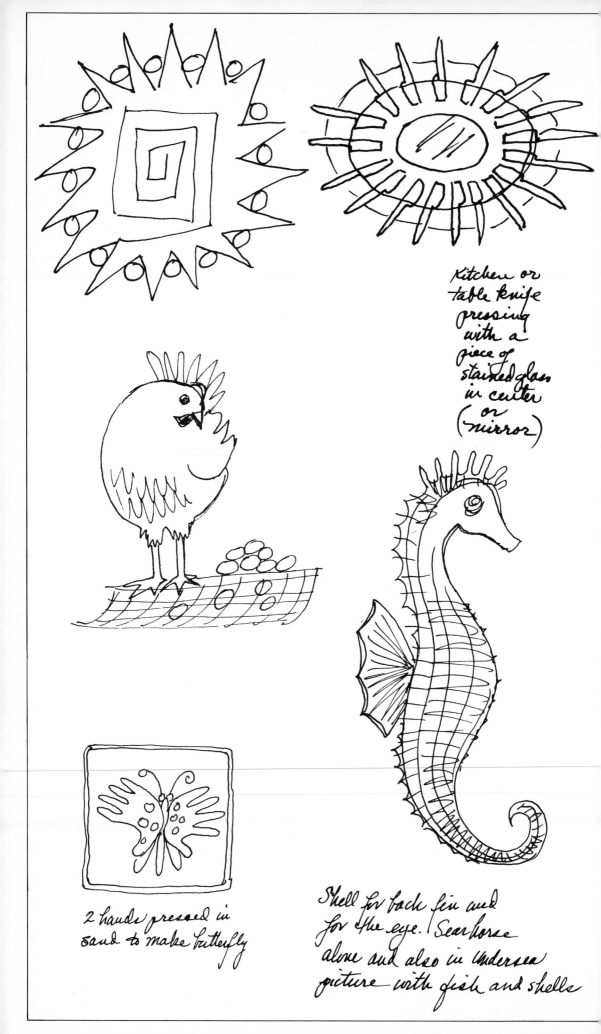

Kitchen or
table knife
pressing
with a
piece of
stained glass
in center
(or
mirror)

2 hands pressed in
sand to make butterfly

Shell for back fin and
for the eye. Seahorse
alone and also in Undersea
picture with fish and shells

animal plaques
or with driftwood
on a block or free-
standing

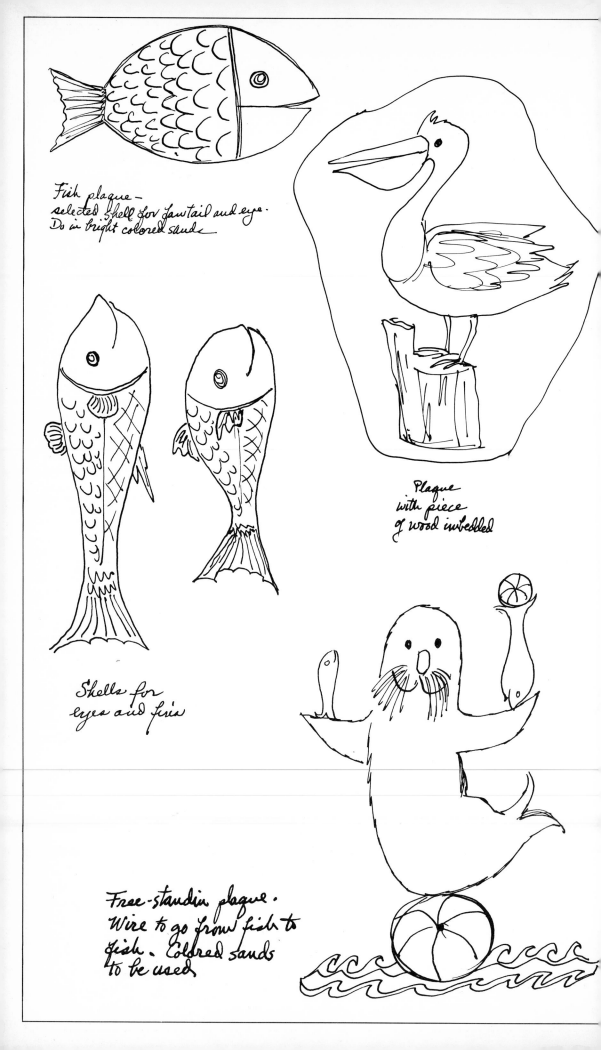

Fish plaque —
selected shell for fantail and eye.
Do in bright colored sands

Plaque
with piece
of wood imbedded

Shells for
eyes and fins

Free-standing plaque.
Wire to go from fish to
fish. Colored sands
to be used

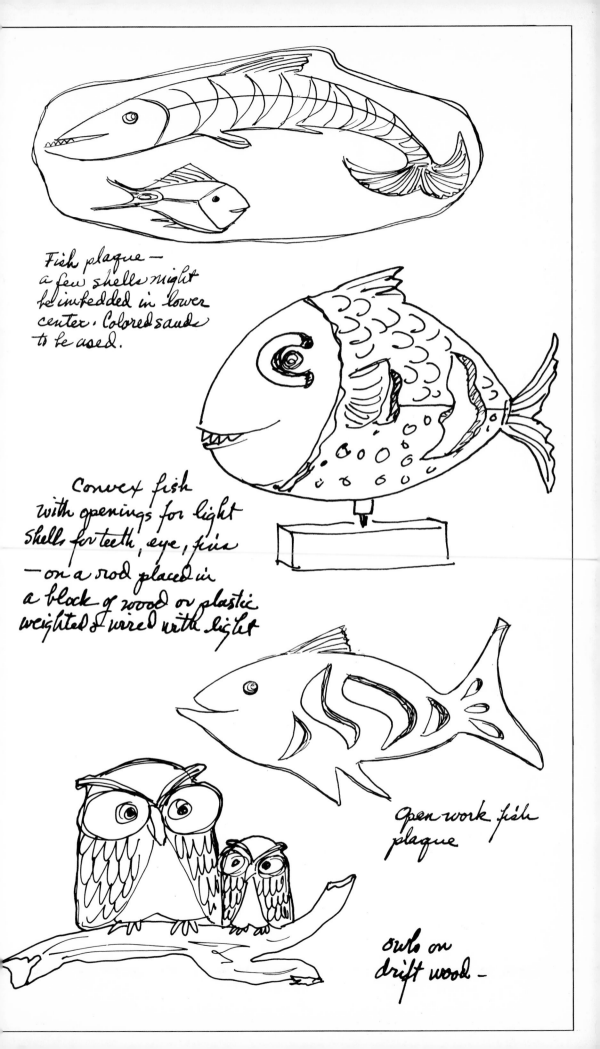

Fish plaque —
a few shells might
be imbedded in lower
center. Colored sands
to be used.

Convex fish
with openings for light
shells for teeth, eye, fins
— on a rod placed in
a block of wood or plastic
weighted & wired with light

Open work fish
plaque

owls on
drift wood —

Plaque. Stained glass to be used in windows and in the doorways.

angel plaque

PHOTO SERIES 25   *A Sketch Becomes A Plaque*

1. The sandbox has been prepared, sand firmly tamped, a depression made for the plaque. The sketch of an angel has been drawn on the sand. The artist strengthens the edge of the border.

2. Portions of the figure have been scooped out to give higher relief. The halo will be formed by a glass sandwich as shown in Photo Series 23. Two halo shapes have been cut from layers of clay. One shape is in place above the angel's head projecting ⅛″ above her hair; the sand around it is being tamped. In the lower right the artist holds the other clay shape pressed firmly against a piece of glass. The glass must project beyond the clay, but it need not be cut accurately to shape.

    The first bit of plaster will be poured over the hair and face of the angel up to the level of the top of the clay surrounding her head; then the glass will be placed on the wet plaster, thus forming the sandwich.

3. Plaster has been poured over the face and into the top portion of the arch. The glass with clay attached is put in place.

4. Pouring has been completed; the back of the plaque is smoothed.

5. Excess plaster is cut away from the back of the halo.

6. The plaster has set, the plaque has been turned over, and excess plaster is removed from the front of the halo. Then the plaque will be washed.

7. Sand is scraped away from the edge of the halo to give it a white rim.

8. The finished plaque (also shown in color).

We hope that sand casting will continue to excite and inspire you, that you will develop your own style—find your own path and follow it, leaving your fingerprints in the sands of time.

Sources Of Supply

Practically everything a sandcaster needs can be purchased at a nearby hobby shop, hardware store, or building-supply dealer—except stained glass (some hobby shops carry it but not all).

General Supplies

American Handicrafts
Chicago Heights, Ill. 60411
> Send for catalog, or look in yellow pages in your area.

A.I. Friedman
25 W. 45th St.
New York, N.Y. 10036
> Send for catalog.

Stained Glass

S.A. Bendheim Co., Inc.
122 Hudson St.
New York, N.Y. 10013
> Catalog free. 10″ x 16″ sheets of glass (by the piece), and scrap glass (by the pound).

Glass Master Guild
621 Ave. of the Americas
New York, N.Y. 10011
> Send for catalog.

Nervo Distributors
650 University Ave.
Berkeley, Calif. 94710
> Catalog $1.00. Sheet glass, glass jewels, scrap glass.

Stained Glass Resources, Inc.
P.O. Box 1442
Salt Lake City, Utah 84110
> No catalog. Ships only 10″ x 10″ sheets of Tiffany glass and other unusual colors, flat price $3.50 each.

Whittemore-Durgin Glass Co.
P.O. Box 2065
Hanover, Mass. 02339
> Catalog free. All materials, kits, etc.

Index